The Life of Your Love

Calling in the Love of Your Life

The Life of Your Love

Calling in the Love of Your Life

Ann Crawford

Lightscapes Publishing
Lakewood, Colorado

© 2026 by Ann Crawford

All rights reserved.

No part of this publication may be reproduced, distributed, or transmitted in any form or by any means, including photocopying, recording, or other electronic or mechanical methods, without the prior written permission of the publisher, except in the case of brief quotations embodied in critical reviews and certain other noncommercial uses permitted by copyright law.

Cover and interior design by Lightscapes Publishing
For permission requests, please contact info@lightscapespublishing.com

ISBN: 978-0-9821690-3-2
Printed in the United States of America
First Edition

This is a work of nonfiction/memoir. Some names and identifying details have been changed.

The information in this book is not intended as medical, psychological, or legal advice.

For
Steve

the love of my life
and the life of my love.
Living this story with you
is the greatest gift of my life.

Table of Contents

Introduction 11

Chapter 1 23
   Calling in a Life Built for Two:
   How to Be an Invitation for Love

Chapter 2 35
   The 12 Steps of Manifestation:
   Becoming Magnetic to Your Love

Chapter 3 73
   Being a Match for the Love You Want:
   Fun Surprises Happen When You
   Get Really Clear

Chapter 4 103
   Love Starts Within:
   The Secret to Becoming the One
   Who Calls in Your Love

Summary 125

Appendix 141

Forgiveness Meditation 149

Recommended Reading................. 151

Acknowledgements 153

Books by Ann Crawford 157

About the Author.......................... 163

Of all the gifts humans have, true love is the greatest gift of all. Love of another is the way to express Infinite Love in all Its Glory.

— from my novel *Spellweaver*

Introduction

You are not only lovable, you are love itself — so you are immeasurably lovable.

Ann Crawford

Welcome to My Little Book of Big Love

Care to know the one thing every book I write has in common? If I write it, you know it'll be a love story — not a romance novel, but more like the *Outlander* kind of love story. I love love. Happy sigh. I think it's the best invention ever.

I want to experience what love is in all its glorious forms. Love of another human being is definitely like knowing what it's like to have The Infinite wrap Its arms around us.

Of course, this love doesn't necessarily have to be with a partner . . . it could be with a parent, a child, a dear friend, a high calling of work, a vision, a purpose, Life Itself.

But this book is about finding the love of your life and the life of your love: the partner you most want to throw your arms around and get to experience what it's like to have The Infinite — Life, Love — wrap Its arms around you. So, welcome to my little book of big love.

As I once said to my husband Steve, "If I heard a life-extinguishing meteor was headed to Earth, I certainly would not want to go home and snuggle up with my books, much as I adore my work!"

What This Book Can Help You Do

I have friends who sincerely don't want relationships. Some do want a relationship, but don't want to compromise at all; so their preference is no relationship. That's totally fine.

But for those who really want that special loving partnership, these pages can help you:

1. Clear old patterns that block deep, soul-aligned love.

2. Strengthen your self-trust and open your heart with confidence.

3. Learn simple spiritual and practical tools for calling in your ideal partner.

4. Prepare yourself for a relationship that uplifts, expands, and supports the highest expression of each of you, on your own and together.

5. Discover how to recognize real partnership, not fantasy or fixation.

6. Deepen your capacity for emotional clarity, forgiveness, and peace.

Soulmates, Podmates, and Twin Flames

In my definition, we have many, many soulmates. To me, soulmates are podmates, people we're meant to swim through life with to do this or that together, people we've swum with before and will again. We have many soulmates in our lifetimes.

We have one twin flame, though (at least one at a time and perhaps for just one season of life, perhaps more): that person who meets us where we're at and provides the foundation for ever-greater growth . . .

That person who enables us to love ourselves even more . . .

That person who loves us into a higher expression of ourselves . . .

That person who enables us to say, "I love me more when I'm with you" . . .

That person who, when we come together, synergizes with us, and our union is lifted to be far greater than the sum of our parts . . .

That person who, when we're in partnership, enables us to serve the world (together and individually) at a greater level than we ever could alone.

> **Our twin flame synergizes with us; our union is lifted to be greater than the sum of its parts.**

I'm all for independence, but in this partnership we feed each other in ways no one else can. Plus, we are fed in ways no other situation can feed us, not even being a fully self-actualized person.

My Own Lessons of Love

It turns out I'm very good at manifesting a very loving husband. Well, let's make that two, anyway, and certainly not at the same time!

They came in for different seasons of my life, one for a large part of my summer season, the other for the long-term, for the late summer, fall, and winter seasons (Life willing). Steve enjoys saying, "I love growing gold with you."

But I'm telling you about the first to let you know I've experienced divorce and heartache — and to let you know Life can shine again after such tough decisions and times. And if you're saying, "Why should I listen to her? She's been divorced. She couldn't even keep her previous spouse." I didn't want to and he didn't either.

It doesn't mean that whole marriage was wrong. Divorce is not a failure — it's just another step on the path, sometimes one of the most important steps.

And many more of my lessons will be shared.

Love That Launches

It takes such a complicated combination of committing to the relationship without losing oneself. But together, Steve and I are galvanized, which launches us into higher ways of being as well as activities that serve the greater good.

> **Together, we're launched in ways that serve the greater good.**

It's more than love because, frankly, I love everyone (although there are some I don't like . . . we can always love the Higher Self or Soul of some folks, but not necessarily want to have lunch with them).

I genuinely *like* Steve, shown by how much I love spending time with him and want to see him happy. Many books about love talk about putting the relationship first . . . but that's only if the relationship serves each individual at this higher level.

Here's one example of many: I've written eight books in the years since I met Steve and just three in my whole life before that. He's joined several bands, and music — one of his major joys — is a bigger part of his life than it was even conceived of before. Those are just two of the myriad ways our partnership uplifts each of us individually and together.

When Healing Becomes the Path

The twin-flame partnership calls for maturity. "Relationship is the biggest game on the planet," to quote spiritual teacher Jim Self.

Alone, we can be kind, compassionate, altruistic, gracious. In relationship, our unhealed "stuff" and our emotional insecurities come out . . . to be revealed — and healed.

In relationship, our unhealed "stuff" and emotional insecurities come out to be revealed — and healed.

This is not a book about healing the deep, deep wounds that have been blocking you from calling in a high-level partner. You are not only lovable, you *are* love itself, and hence immeasurably lovable. If you have any doubts about that, you can get them worked out.

There are plenty of books about healing those internal injuries (please see my Recommended Reading list at the end of the book). Without that recovery, we all tend to just keep clashing, both inside and out, until we face those hurts and heal them.

Ann Crawford

A dear friend — Peter Tork of The Monkees fame, as a matter of fact — once said when we change partners, we change the battlefield but not the battle. That is, until we heal our inner battle.

I reminded him of his wise words later, and he remarked, "I said that? I'm pretty smart!" (He wasn't funny only in the TV show.)

If you're with someone who feels the need to tear or pull you down, leave until they've healed that and you've healed the need to be with someone who doesn't honor you fully. If you feel the need to tear people down, leave them alone and go heal that. It's a self-love issue.

You don't have to talk anyone into loving you. You don't have to chase after anyone with a butterfly net. True love meets halfway, and it never has to be pushed or prodded.

True love meets halfway. It never has to be chased or prodded.

A Light, Playful Guide for Big Love

When I was hesitating about putting this book out — because my life certainly isn't perfect — my husband said, "But your relationship is!"

Humble, isn't he? Yes, he was definitely joking.

And while it's not perfect all the time, as he says, "You have what most people in the world are looking for, what everybody wishes they had. You've accomplished what could be one of the most important aspects of life — having a deep, loving relationship with another person who absolutely adores you. And vice versa."

Sound good? Okay then — you can have this, too. Let's get on that.

This book is meant to be light, uplifting, and upbeat for when a chunk of the inner healing has been done . . . although the full healing is the work of a lifetime, literally.

Ann Crawford

If partnership with your twin flame is what you're after, here are a few fun ideas and a playful tale that might inspire you.

So much love,
Ann
Colorado 2026

Chapter 1
Calling in a Life Built for Two: How to Be an Invitation for Love

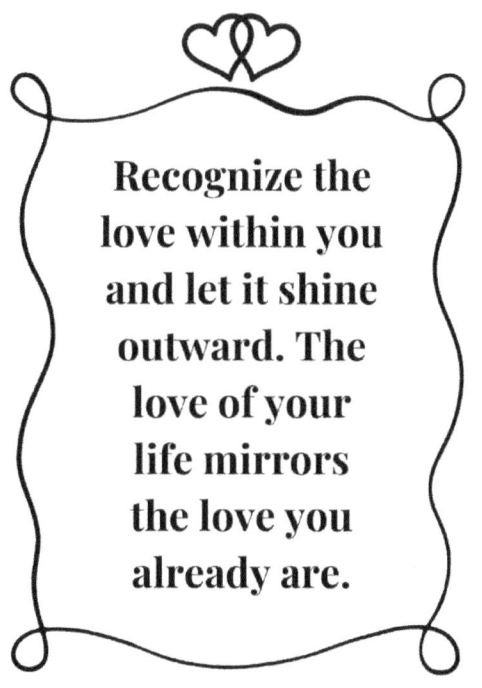

Recognize the love within you and let it shine outward. The love of your life mirrors the love you already are.

♥

Brian and I decided early on in our relationship, we would make decisions based on not what does Arielle want or what does Brian want, but rather on "what most serves the relationship."

We share our "stuff" with each other, not just the physical stuff, but the stuff of our core emotional issues. We are open, transparent, vulnerable with each other and "own" when our "stuff" is getting in the way or when we need support on something.

It's not easy, sometimes scary, but we believe what author Harville Hendrix teaches: "The true purpose of marriage is to heal our childhood wounds." Having a partner who is open, willing, and a safe place to land provides the greatest healing possible.

Arielle Ford & Brian Hilliard
Married for 28 years.[1]
Their love story is described
in Arielle's amazing book
The Soulmate Secret.

♥

Declare and Accept

My friends have long called me an amazing, master manifester. In fact, when Steve and I got married, a friend's wedding gift was a statue of a man and woman, à la Oscar, and she said, "Now presenting, the Amazing Manifester Award!"

One time when I was twenty-seven, a friend asked, "What do you want?"

It was one of *those* moments. "More than anything in the world," I answered, "I want to go around the world."

She didn't tell me I was crazy or to get serious, that kind of thing. Instead she said, "Get your passport. Write your itinerary." The next thing I knew I was headed off around the world.

Before I left, another friend asked, "What do you want out of this trip?"

"A husband!"

I was kidding (kind of), but Life took me quite seriously. To paraphrase the metaphysical philosopher and author Florence Scovel Shinn, Life always takes us at our most fully intended word — It doesn't joke. I came home with a husband.

Speaking of Life taking us literally, I once recommended a group at a spiritual center stop calling itself "Singles," when they were actually looking for partners. That name in itself is an affirmation, pretty much.

> **Life always takes us at our most fully intended word.**

When my previous marriage had run its course and we'd outgrown each other, I became very clear about what I wanted: "a husband, a family, and a home filled with love, light, and laughter." Then, very quickly, love arrived — with family gathered, joy overflowing, laughter on repeat.

The Life of Your Love

♥

Laugh a lot. Be best friends. Don't sweat the small stuff. Live independent lives, but make sure you stay connected.

Karen & Paul
Married for 32 years.
They met as next-door neighbors.

♥

These quotes scattered throughout the book are from couples I know. I told them, "I'm writing a book about finding the love of your life. With one exception, I'm asking couples who've been married for 10+ years (and it looks like it'll keep on keepin' on), what one or two secrets do you think add to your happiness as a couple as well as your ability to stay together?"

While one friend chuckled at my 70s reference, they were all eager to tell me. I love their responses, which are wonderfully salt of the earth. My answer is really this whole book, plus I have a flip, fun one near the end.

Ann Crawford

When Love Came to Town

Steve and I were matched on eHarmony on June 21, 2006. We met face to face on July 14. We were engaged on July 16. I had my little green Prius packed up and was moving from my little hippie surfer town on the Northern California coast to Topeka, Kansas, on July 21. And, oh, did I mention he had two teenagers at the time?

I know, I know — I hear what you're saying. He could've been a serial killer or a con artist or something along those lines. But so could someone I met at the gym, in a country club, or on the airport shuttle. (I have two friends who met that way and eventually married). Everyone needs to be checked out, no matter where we find them.

The night before I was going to fly to Kansas City to meet him in person for the first time, he asked me if I was sure about him.

"I'm 93 percent sure," I said.

"Uh, 93?"

"Well, it's more than 90 and less than 95." For a wordsmith, I'm quite the numbers person, too.

He still teases me about that. He was 100 percent sure. "You had me at Ann," he loves to say. (Their name is the first thing we see on a potential match's eH profile, of course.)

I love to tease Steve: "You had me at Joel."

Steve mentioned on his profile that the most influential person in his life is the spiritual teacher and author Joel Goldsmith. Now, while millions of Goldsmith's books have sold, he is very esoteric and not many in the mainstream culture have heard of him. But I'd definitely heard of him and read a fair bit of his work.

My eyebrows flew up to my hairline, and my heart skipped a beat because I recognized a spiritual soul. I love to tease Steve: "You had me at Joel."

And then I burst into his life, as he also loves to say.

Falling in love took a minute. Getting to that minute took decades.

♥

For me, number one is laughter. Second is patience. Lucky for me, I love to laugh and have always had the patience of Job!

Stephen & Rob
Consciously Coupled for 34 years,
married as long as it's
been legal in New York.
They met at a cocktail party.

Love with a Larger Purpose

I've done many workshops based on my book *Visioning*. Some workshops were for visioning your twin flame/calling in the love of your life.

One of the most important questions in the workshop for general visioning is, "Why *don't* you want your dream to come true?" For visioning the love of your life, the question is, "Why *don't* you want the love of your life?"

The answer reveals much of what we need to know. Perhaps it's because we're valuing independence and our current lifestyle over partnership. Perhaps it's fear. Whatever the answer is, that's the area calling for a shift or healing.

Another part of my workshop includes forgiveness: beFORe we can give, we have to FORgive. A sample forgiveness meditation is included in the Appendix, and the audio version is on my website (address at end of book).

Another thing I ask in my workshops is, "How does this serve?" How does this dream, relationship, partnership, serve the greater good? Asking this question lifts the union or dream up to its highest outlook and biggest purpose.

How does this relationship serve the greater good?

This is also part of writing a Sacred Covenant, which you can do for a partnership. (Sacred Covenants were developed by Revs. Lloyd Strom and Marcia Sutton, whose teachings continue to inspire. These Covenants are explored in Chapter 7 of *Visioning*.) "What is the highest outlook for this union, business, project, or life? What are you, or the union, or business, or project alive for?"

Author and futurist Barbara Marx Hubbard often wrote about co-creative couples — those of us who unite to do big work together for the good of all. She believed the love-energy of these special pairs could even help evolve humanity itself.

♥

He held space for my wildness — it was a big job.

Betsey & George
Together 27 years when he passed.
He was the minister at the church she attended.

♥

From a single friend:

I want to be fully empowered and have reassurance that it's going to happen even if it's not happening yet. I don't want to be told to give up on what I want — I *will* get it. I want to reinforce being clear about what I want and not compromising. It's very upsetting when people say I'm asking too much, to lower my standards. No way!

Chapter 2
The 12 Steps of Manifestation: Becoming Magnetic to Your Love

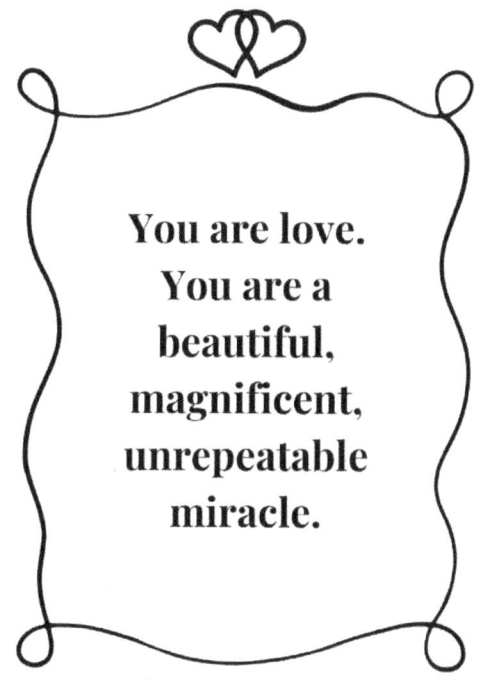

You are love. You are a beautiful, magnificent, unrepeatable miracle.

The Most Important Question

This chapter is dedicated to manifesting in general, and then I'll get back to the topic of love in particular.

A very dear friend of mine, a minister and master metaphysical teacher, once asked me, "What do you think is the most important question?" I'll share my first answer to that question with you at the end of this chapter.

But my second answer, which was geared to a much wider audience and to include new spiritual seekers, was, "So, how's your life going?" Because if someone's life is going great, then great. If it's not going great, then it can get great. And here's how.

The 12 Steps of Manifestation

There are 12 Steps of Manifestation. This isn't a borrowed list; it's a lived one.

- Step 1: Know that Love is the only power there is.

- Step 2: Do your own inner spiritual work and awaken.

- Step 3: Know that everything is energy and vibration.

- Step 4: Know that thought is creative.

- Step 5: Be *crystal clear* about what you want.

- Step 6: Know that feelings are the power behind manifestation.

- Step 7: Forgive and move on.

Step 8: Reciprocity — giving and receiving — is how the Universe works.

Step 9: Follow the path of least resistance.

Step 10: Make sure what you want and the way you're going about it are for the good of all and the harm of none.

Step 11: Let go and let the Universe handle it — and don't give up before the miracle happens.

Step 12: Life is ultimately about love and service.

Step 1: Know that Love is the only power there is.

Love is the only power there is . . . . Anywhere . . . . Everywhere. To me, God, Life, and Love are synonymous. Love is the power that lights up and animates every atom in all of creation. And if Love is all there is, that's all we are, too.

Do you love yourself? Actually, it's even beyond loving yourself — you *are* love. That's who and what you are. *You are love.* You are love in form, love in a body, love with a smile, love sitting in a chair reading these words.

Love is the only power there is. That's who you are.

You are a living, moving, walking, breathing, smiling center of Life. Yes, you, and the person next to you, and the person next to them, and the person next to them — although you can really tell who knows it now and who will come to know it at some point in the future.

That's what the great masters have always taught. Self-love is recognizing this bigger Love.

Step 2: Do your own inner spiritual work and awaken.

Yes, we are beautiful, magnificent, unrepeatable miracles — and there's always room for improvement. It may be called spiritual *work*, but it's not drudgery.

The exploration of the inner landscape can be one of the most rewarding voyages of life. We have to do our own spiritual work, but that doesn't mean we have to do it on our own. We're all here for each other.

> **The exploration of the inner landscape can be one of the most rewarding voyages of life.**

Here are just some of the tools we can use in our spiritual work: therapy, spiritual counseling, spiritual studies, daily prayer and meditation (emphasis on *daily*), affirmations, praise phrase (a positive line or word to run over and over in your head when the less-than-positive mantras want to take over), breathwork, love-and-light practices, physical fitness routines, spiritual fellowship and community, service to others, creative expression/art, and journaling.

We can tell how much more physically fit we are by how quickly our heartbeat returns to normal after an exertion. The same is true for spiritual fitness.

Spiritual mastery is not how well we can *avoid* life's tribulations — because no one can, and they're often important parts of the journey. The mastery is in how quickly we can return to our center in the midst of them.

Step 3: Know that everything is energy and vibration.

Everything — every moment, every situation — comes about because of us. We attract what we are, what we're vibrating at.

Want to call something into your life? *Vibrate at that level.* That means living, even in small ways, as if what you desire is already true — showing up with the confidence, gratitude, openness, or joy that matches the thing you're calling in. When our actions, emotions, and expectations line up with what we want, Life rises to meet us there.

Want something out of your life? *Vibrate higher and everything unlike it will fade away.* Raising your vibration isn't about pretending to be happy; it's about choosing thoughts and habits that expand you rather than contract you.

Want something in your life? Vibrate at that level. Don't want something? Vibrate higher and it'll fall away.

As you do that, people, situations, and patterns that don't resonate with your new frequency simply can't stick. They loosen, drift off, or transform — sometimes gently, sometimes not so much, sometimes miraculously.

It's not fate. It's not karma. It's not what we've done. It's all consciousness. Our consciousness is the set of beliefs and ideas we hold. Often the very thing we're looking for comes from *being* the very thing we're looking for. If we want peace, we practice being peaceful. If we want love, we offer love. If we want clarity, we cultivate stillness.

> **Often what we're looking for comes from *being* what we're looking for.**

It's not about chasing things outside of ourselves. It's about embodying them so fully the outer world can't help but mirror them back.

We don't have to ask for anything. Everything we could possibly want has already been given to us, in abundance. *We just step into it.*

That "stepping in" is an inner shift where we loosen the old beliefs that say we're not ready or not worthy, and we let ourselves receive what's been waiting for us all along. Life isn't withholding; often we're just learning how to open the door.

Life isn't withholding; often we're just learning how to open the door.

We don't just have intelligence; we *are* one with the intelligence of the Universe. We don't need abundance; we *are* the flow of abundance personified. We don't call in health; we allow the health we already are to flow through our being. We don't just have beauty; we are beauty. We aren't looking for love; we are love.

Step 4: Know that thought is creative.

Life is *your* tapestry to weave, your picture to paint, your script to write, your sculpture to mold. It's that literal. The universe responds to your thought like potter's clay, like a canvas, like a loom, like plastic.

> **The Universe responds to your thoughts like potter's clay, canvas, a loom, plastic.**

Your thoughts create your experience. As you think, so is your life. For a glimpse at what you were thinking yesterday, look at your life today. How's it working out for you? You can change your thoughts accordingly.

A friend of mine once said, "I wish I could see some previews of coming attractions for my life."

"You can," I responded. "Just think them up!"

In *Visioning*, I mentioned a friend was always going to a psychic. I finally said to her, "Why don't you decide what you want, and then go tell the psychic how it's all going to turn out?"

She burst into tears and said, "Because I don't think I deserve what I want!"

Well, now we're getting somewhere. Realizing an inner belief like that is hiding out in there — launching firebombs at anything resembling joy — is over half the journey to healing that condition.

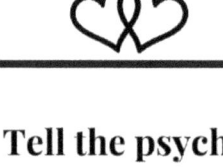

Tell the psychic how it's going to turn out.

This is nothing against psychics. They have a tremendous gift to give, especially when we get stuck. But she seemed to be relying on them and not doing her inner work in conjunction.

And, of course, my friends say similar things to me in those moments when I forget what's Real. That famous AA saying goes, "This program works because we're not all crazy all the time."

The thoughts between the prayers count as much, because those are prayers, too.

Thoughts not only create things, thoughts *are* things. Every thought you've ever had has produced *something* — whether it was extra poundage on your body or a svelte figure; a good experience at a bad job or a bad experience at a good job; sickness or health; physical well-being or illness; success or something less.

It's not necessarily just the formal prayers that bring in what we wish to manifest: it's the thoughts between the prayers, which are also prayers in themselves. And often these are far more powerful than formal prayers, because they are wrapped up in emotion . . . but more about that in Step 6.

Every thought is a prayer, and every prayer is answered. I'm not talking about beseeching, more like making a declaration. So, every declaration — in one way or another, at one level or another, in that realm where energy responds to energy — comes with an answer. Each prayer is met with a response that matches its resonance: an immediate nudge, a sign that appears much later, a doorway, a feeling, perhaps a gentle redirect.

Energy responds to energy; each prayer receives a corresponding resonance.

The answers aren't always on our timeline or bubble-wrapped in the packaging we expect. But they arrive all the same through the quiet intelligence of Life — sometimes in a way that serves us even better than what we asked for.

When we open to money or a job or a mate, we can align with the ideas, suggestions, and inspirations that allow us to vibrate at the level of all we want to attract into our lives. The Universe's job is to say yes to that which we impress upon it, call in, intend. So if we think the main outpicturing of our lives is not what we had in mind, then we need to take a closer look at what we truly have in our mind.

Clarity can be a great magnet.

Step 5: Be *crystal clear* about what you want.

Clarity can be a great magnet. Muddled thoughts beget muddled results. Clarity — along with taking the action steps we're guided to take and then getting out of the way to let the Universe get to it — will call in our dreams.

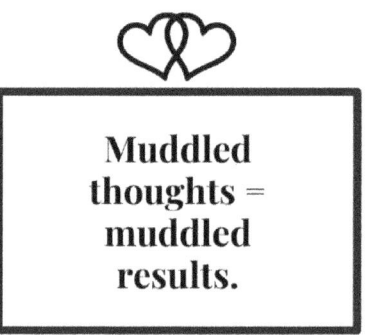

Tools for getting clear include those listed in Step 2 plus: set your intention; write it out clearly again and again; join goal groups, support groups, or mastermind circles; create treasure maps and vision boards (collages); make a list and read it frequently; tell someone. In fact, tell everyone.

The vision board I made the January before I met Steve includes a wedding ring and a family of four. Vision boards are extremely powerful!

You know how when we're under water, we can't see clearly at all, and a dull roaring sound fills our ears, and we can't breathe? And yet, if we just stick our head out of the water, we'll see a bright blue sky, hear children laughing and waves crashing, and be able to — aaahhhhhhhhhhhh — breathe?

That's what stopping for prayer, meditation, and other tools for clarity does for our lives. It lifts us out of the opaque vantage point, the ear-filling dull roar, the breath-stopping filler of the world, and it returns us to heightened clarity on all levels.

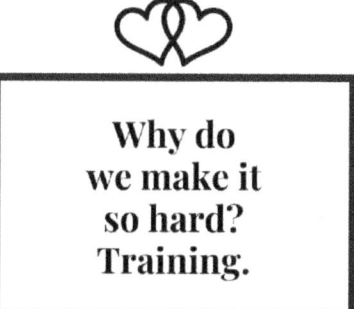

Why do we make it so hard? Training.

Why do we make it so hard? Our early training. We were trained by people who didn't know any better, who were also trained by people who didn't know any better, who were . . . . You get the picture.

But the true nature of life — of *L*ife and of us — is to grow, expand, and express more and more and more of itself. More love, more joy, more abundance, more harmony, more order, more light.

That true nature ultimately prevails. We pop our head out of the water — the illusion, the roar, the suffocation of our limited consciousness — and breathe, at last.

What we are most passionate about is what materializes.

Step 6: Know that feelings are the power behind manifestation.

As I mention in Step 3, every thought is a prayer. They are sometimes far more powerful than formal prayers, because our random thoughts can be packed with feelings outside our conscious awareness. The things we are most passionate about are what materialize — and too often we're very passionate about what we fear, which is why too often we bring our greatest fears upon ourselves.

> **When we're anchored in Life, fear might whisper, but it can't shut off the flow anymore.**

Fear is an automatic constrictor. It's like stepping on the garden hose without realizing it and wondering why the plants are still thirsty. We're beings of such tremendous love and light . . . and yet so many of us are standing on our own garden hose surrounded by withered flowers of our own making.

Fear can be a wonderful gift, too, however, because it can sometimes push faith into our lives. When we're anchored in faith, in Life, it's as if we finally step off the hose — fear might still whisper, but it can't shut off the flow anymore. Anchored in faith, the possibilities are infinite.

Resentments clog the channels, both figuratively and literally.

Step 7: Forgive and move on.

Forgive and move on . . . . Everyone is doing the best they can at any particular time. It might not be the best they can ever do, but it's their best given their consciousness in that one moment.

The only person you're hurting by holding onto grudges is yourself. A plane can't fly if it's loaded down with ice, a metaphor for resentments frozen in place.

Forgiveness is not for the benefit of the other person; it is for us. The other person benefits, too, of course, since everything is interconnected.

But the main reason we forgive is for us. Plus, it's the higher path — a much higher good than holding onto resentment, no matter how intense the reason to hold onto it is. Resentments clog the channels, both figuratively and literally: in the world we create all around us as well as in our bodies, where stuck emotions can turn into sickness.

Sometimes the main person we could forgive is ourselves.

To create a visionary life of choice, we have to clear our sluiceways. A major way this happens is by cleaning up our own misdeeds as well as letting go of the misdeeds of others, both past and present.

Sometimes the main person we have to forgive is ourselves — for not knowing more or doing "better" way back when or even this morning. One person in the "everyone is doing the best they can at any particular time" is us.

And sometimes we even have to forgive Life — for seemingly taking someone too soon, for cataclysmic events, for other circumstances outside of anyone's control. "Life happens" is not just a trite phrase.

BeFORe we can give, we have to FORgive. Even Life. That's for us, though all benefit.

Again, beFORe we can give, we must FORgive. Our lives will be the better for it, and our bodies will love us for it.

Step 8: Reciprocity — giving and receiving, cause and effect — is how the Universe works.

Everything is a cycle: the seasons, the path of the Earth around the sun. Giving and receiving are the cycle of life.

We must create a vacuum to receive, however, and we must give from a place of being filled up to overflowing. We can't give from an empty well. But as soon as possible, we could start giving *something* to get the flow going — even a smile, a compliment, or a favor.

Want more love? Give more love. We receive at the level we give.

> **Want more love?
> Give more love.
> We receive at the
> level we give.**

Step 9: Follow the path of least resistance.

This does *not* always mean the easiest way. Challenges can be an important part of the journey — a polishing of the jewel, which only happens with friction.

But the path for you is the one that's most lit up for you: the way water would run downhill in your life, the way that seems lightest, the way that ignites passion and joy. If you feel like you're carrying a boulder up a hill in the black of night, chances are this isn't the right road.

> **The path for you is the one that's most lit up for you.**

There's a soft, easy gentleness around the things that manifest easily. There's no efforting, there's no forcing, there's no pushing, there's no *making* things happen. There's no bending iron with brute force or pushing boulders uphill. There's right timing. There's heart-based desire. And there's love.

The people and situations that are not called in as a result of love — but are called in from fear, greed, ego-based desire — are not people and situations for our highest good, nor do we want to keep them in our lives.

> **If everyone did this, would it serve humanity and the planet?**

Step 10: Make sure what you want and the way you're going about it is for the good of all and the harm of none.

The simple question to ask is this: if everyone did this, would it serve humanity and the planet? You can call in whatever life you desire . . . but if you make it a life of loving service, that will uplift you and everyone around you.

> **Don't give up before the miracle. The still, small voice will tell us if we're on the right path.**

Step 11: Let go and let the Universe handle it — and don't give up before the miracle happens.

We've heard people say, "I wasn't even looking for a wife when I found her!" Or we've often heard about people trying to get pregnant for years, and as soon as they decide to adopt, they get pregnant . . . because the pressure is off.

And the last thing we want to do is give up before the miracle happens. The still, small voice we hear in meditation, walking in nature, doing a spiritual practice, or sitting quietly will tell us if we're on the right path.

In the meantime, we can vision and affirm, which can be like trying on a magnificent garment you don't feel you deserve yet. The more you put it on, though, the more comfortable it will feel. At last you'll know the garment belongs to you — yours by right of consciousness.

The idea is to have our life so filled to overflowing that the desire isn't even the icing on the cake. It's the beautiful red rose on the icing on the cake.

**We have two responsibilities:
1) Evolve our soul.
2) Be a beneficial presence.**

Step 12: Life is ultimately about love and service.

We really only have two responsibilities in this life of ours:

1) Evolve our soul.
2) Be a beneficial presence.

The first part is taken care of. Everything we do — every single thing, in every single moment — evolves our soul. We can't do it wrong. It can be messy, loud, quiet, fraught with failure (although nothing is ever really a failure, just another step on the path), juicy, ugly, sad. But we can't do it wrong. (I mean, within reason — heinous criminal acts not included, although forgiveness can certainly happen there, too.) And we also can't avoid it, because there's nothing else *to* do.

Life always meets us where we are in consciousness.

We can, however, get tired of the same old mess and ugliness and call in a higher experience. "Love lifts us higher" is not just a cute phrase from a song, but the very nature of Creation.

Life always meets us where we are in consciousness. As for some of the bad stuff? Nelson Mandela kept and grew his higher consciousness in prison.

And once we call in a higher experience, we can be the second part of the two-part program of Life: a beneficial presence. Generously share your wisdom, wealth, bounty, time, talent, and treasure.

Everything we do can be acts of serving, loving, and revering.

So, everything in life is a prelude, a working for, or a result of these two things . . . which means life ultimately is about love and service. Everything we do can be an act of love, service, and reverence for Life.

The Buddhist monk Thich Nhat Hanh used to recommend washing dishes as if we were washing the baby Buddha. Just imagine how much our lives would change if we gave every task that much reverence.

Even if it's working a job temporarily and doing your creative endeavor at night and on Saturday afternoons, you are loving, serving, and revering. And you can pray, invoke, and prepare the way for bigger success.

The Answer

Okay, here's the first answer to that question my dear friend asked me, as I promised back in the beginning of this chapter. The most important question to ask is, "Am I in my High Self right now?" Because if we are in our High Self, then all is well, Life flows, things can manifest easily. If we are not in our High Self, though, we can always get back there.

How do we know when the answer is yes? If all is truly well in our heart, no matter what the external circumstances are, the answer is yes. (I didn't say it'd always be easy!) And when the answer is yes, our external circumstances fall into line, too.

Bending with the Winds of Change

Manifesting is not about bulldozing through life, or being like a mighty oak tree . . . it's more like being a willow — firmly planted but able to bend with the winds of change, the vicissitudes of life. We have it in us. Our mighty potential lives within, like the mighty oak already lives within the acorn.

When we run out of steam, it's because we've been pushing with our own energy. (Steve would gently ask, though, "Should we make a stop at the steam store?")

But when we tap into the stillness of the center, where the all-powerful energy resides, it's impossible to run out of steam. Steam — Energy, Life — is all there is!

Have you ever noticed that sometimes we've been running around the house — and our lives — trying to accomplish as much as possible? Accomplishing as much as possible is not the point.

The point isn't how much we get done; it's how much love we get it done with.

The point is not racing through the grocery store to get it done quickly . . . the point is smiling back at the lonely man we pass in the aisle or at the checkout person. The point isn't eating dinner . . . it's tasting it. The point isn't getting the job done . . . it's how much reverence we show in the process.

It's better to do less with more love than the other way around. And it's never what we do or say that matters as much as how we live our lives.

And I'm not just talking about manifesting *things*. Things are just that — the added things, which Jesus assured us would come when we focus on the Divine within.

Demonstration starts with the spiritual, and then the form easily follows. Our consciousness of the Divinity within ourselves — including our awareness *of* our awareness — is the greatest gift. Everything else falls into place.

And the winner is . . . not the one who does the most or gets the most, but the one who does whatever it is they do with the most love. It's also the one who most appreciates what they manifest. And what they're giving is what they're getting.

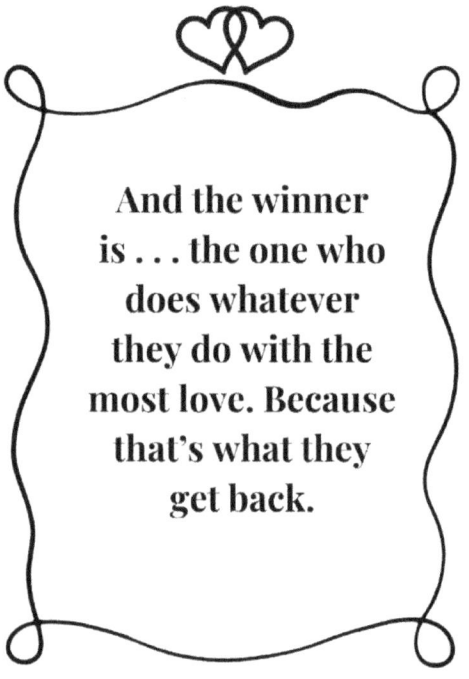

And the winner is . . . the one who does whatever they do with the most love. Because that's what they get back.

The Life of Your Love

Already

We are the love —
Twin flame right there, or no one.
Love can take so many different forms,
With or without the relationship

We are the beauty —
Whether dreary day or radiant sun,
Rose or thorn,
Anywhere we are.

We are the joy —
Doing the dishes or making love,
Cradling a baby or commuting,
Tending to a tedious task or
witnessing the accomplishment
of a lifetime.

If we are those things,
It doesn't matter what we have
in hand or sight,
Because we already have them
in our heart.

We already *are* them.

And so they're ours,
Long before anything we're awaiting
arrives.

Ann Crawford

We *are* love, beauty, and joy. So we already have everything we're waiting for.

The Life of Your Love

♥

Be and stay friends. Engage with each other and do things together. Be mindful of your passionate life. Keep things physical and connected. If you have kids, don't just be co-parents — remain lovers.

Maya & Luis
Married for 40 years.
They lived on the same
dorm floor in college.

♥

Chapter 3
Being a Match for the Love You Want: Fun Surprises Happen When You Get Really Clear

We attract vibrational matches. Become what you're looking for.

When I knew I was ready for my partner, suddenly in everything I did, I said to myself and the Universe, "I'm doing this to bring in my person." When I did a firewalk, my intention was, "I'm walking to find my true love." When I burned a piece of flash paper, to send a message out to the Universe in a New Year's ritual, I said the same thing, "I'm ready to find my true love." I did that with everything.

I did not let up on the creative law. I kept looking, asking, querying, making connections, and not getting discouraged. I upped it right before I met Paul.

I wasn't wistful. I kept saying, "Now is the time, now is the time." I didn't let up.

Paul said it was love at first sight. I knew instantly, too, and I said to myself, "I am going to say yes to anything this man suggests."

Karyl & Paul
Married for eight years.
They met online and
moved to England.

The Life of Your Love

LoveLoveLoveLove and the Creative Law

Okay, now, about my favorite topic — loveloveloveloveloveloveloveloveloveloveove lovelove — and, in particular, the process Steve and I took to get there. All of this is also known as the creative law, as Karyl mentions above.

Steve's Timetable

On July 4, 2004, the day after his divorce was final, Steve wrote out a list of traits he wanted in his next — and his last — wife.

People have very different reactions to these lists . . . some say don't make them, some say keep them short. Well, Steve's list included forty items — one-third physical, one-third emotional/intellectual, and one-third spiritual.

1. Female*
2. Tall — between 5'10" and 6'.
3. Athletic body — not too thin, not too fat.
4. Dark hair.
5. Medium-long hair.
6. Blue eyes that sparkle.

7. Long, long legs.
8. Beautiful smile.
9. Intelligent, educated, well read.
10. Positive attitude.
11. Understands the meaning of life: spiritually aware.
12. Sense of humor.
13. Infectious laugh.
14. Likes to have fun.
15. A face so pretty it doesn't need makeup.
16. Uninhibited.
17. Loves music.
18. Never gets sick.
19. A voice I love listening to.
20. Will try anything at least once.
21. No vices — smoking, drugs, alcohol, gambling, food, etc.
22. Success-oriented.
23. Strong beliefs.
24. Enthusiasm for life.
25. Passionate.
26. Sense of purpose.
27. Good imagination.
28. Disciplined.
29. Patient.
30. Kind.
31. High integrity.
32. Pursues excellence.
33. Perseveres — never gives up.

34. Able to see the big picture.
35. Courageous.
36. Very open to giving and receiving love.
37. At peace with her world.
38. Has unconditional and unlimited love for me.
39. Allows me to give her unconditional and unlimited love.
40. Has her own list and I meet every criterion.

*Sometimes the Universe loves to tease us, so he wanted to be specific about this!

When we came together, we meshed so well it was practically unbelievable. Plus, I was almost everything on his list. In fact, we were so stunned at the accuracy — I'm 5'11" and I don't have just long legs, I actually do have long, long legs — that we imagined teams of angels trying to match us.

And that was the impetus for my romantic comedy novel *Angels on Overtime*: thinking about a crazy conversation that a hapless, hard-working team of angels might've had trying to get the two of us together . . . across many miles and around a whole bunch of *very* strange situations. Just for the record, though, Sam, the ex-husband in the book, was way, way worse than mine.

Following is that scene as we imagined it. This part comes through story; you can take it in if you enjoy that kind of thing, or move on without missing a beat.

"So," Brooke announces to the rest of the group, ". . . he wants a wife. Not just any wife — he has a list of forty things there."

"Forty!" Sapphire frowns. "No one ever makes a list of forty qualities in a mate. That'd be impossible."

"Nothing's impossible," Blake reminds her.

"The qualities on the list are about one-third physical, one-third emotional and intellectual, and one-third spiritual," Brooke continues. "And he's crystal, crystal clear about it all. Plus, he's willing to wait for the whole enchilada, even until the next lifetime if he has to. But his work and healing show he's ready for her now. So the question is, how are we

going to find someone who fits all those things?"

Christopher reads each quality on the list aloud and types it into his computer. "Long hair. Beautiful. Intelligent. At peace with her world. Conscious. Has done her work. Not too fussy, is he?" Christopher starts to enter the next requisite attribute but stops. "Six feet tall. Is he over six feet tall? I guess he is, now that he's standing up straight." He finishes entering the information on his laptop and presses the return key.

As the new information appears on the screen, Blake studies it carefully. "Well," he says, "it looks like there's a woman in Idaho who matches every one of these things. Only one problem."

"What's that?" Brooke asks.

"She's married."

"Married! That's obviously not going to work." Brooke pauses for a moment. "Well, how married?"

Blake studies the screen. "Hmmmm, a tiny, tiny spark of love is still there, but the two are no longer a suitable team. They're not on each other's ballpark, I mean wavelength, and not interested in the same game anymore."

After writing that list, though, Steve let it go for a long while.

♥

Invest in each other by celebrating each other's strengths. Surprise each other with tokens of love.

Sue & Steve
Married for 21 years.
Met when introduced
by mutual friends.

♥

My Timetable

On the day Steve wrote out that list, almost 2,000 miles away, I suddenly started talking to the unseen beings around me. Really — I remember I was standing in my bedroom probably looking like I was talking to myself, and it was on the 4th of July.

"Alright already! If you want (my former spouse) and me to be done, you're going to have to handle it, because I'm not leaving. I made a commitment and I'd see it through. But if this relationship no longer serves us at our highest level, do something about it and make it clear as a bell."

A couple months later, an eHarmony ad came on the radio as he and I were driving home. I heard Dr. Neil Clark Warren, the founder of the site, say, "A lot of happy couples out there tonight."

I found myself feeling wistful, wondering if I could be happier and then having the seemingly surprising, sudden realization that I probably could. This all came after seeing a couple's counselor and exploring other avenues, as well.

"Hmmmmm," I thought, "if he and I ever break up, I'm going to join eHarmony." And then I thought, "Well, that's certainly a very strange thought to be having!"

It's amazing the machinations our minds can go through — back and forth, back and forth. This was after having that very clear talk with the Universe two months prior, so it shouldn't have come as such a big surprise, but it still did.

I noticed he was being very quiet, and I asked him if he was okay. We then started the conversation that ended our marriage. It was time, much as I hadn't wanted to admit it to myself.

About a year later, after a healing storm or two or a hundred, I wrote out my list:

- Oneness — connected to the All. A spiritual powerhouse.
- Committed to me, marriage, and family. Has plenty of time and space in his life for us.*
- Joyous, positive, upbeat, clear.
- Physically attractive, healthy, and takes excellent care of himself.

- Responsible, mature, has integrity, financially set.

*I'd dated a few fellows who were "so totally busy." I was so totally done with that. But they obviously weren't the right ones anyway, and their busy-ness was my first clue.

Since I don't live in Tibet or have a horse ...

Plus, there came this from a very dear, spiritual master of a friend of mine: "Ann! When a woman in Tibet wants to find a husband from her village, she jumps on a horse, rides as fast as she can, and the man who can keep up with her is the one for her!" I have no idea if that's actually true or not, but I love the image.

A friend looked at my list and said, "Don't you want to add anything else?"

I added, "Tall and built." And then, "Long hair. Funny, great sense of humor, loves to laugh, makes me laugh a lot." And later, "Knows all the words to 'Thunder Road.'" And even later, "Knows which fork to use."

Another friend looked at my list and said, "You need to become all of these things first, of course."

Of course. We attract vibrational matches. Some of those things I already was and still am. Tall, yes; built, hopefully not so much in the way I meant for him to be, LOL.

Clear out the Clutter, Put Symbolic Items in Twos

I also went full feng shui on the situation: I always had two roses and two red candles in the relationship corner of my house, my bedroom, and my office at work. I even had Barbie and Ken together in their wedding attire! (I read somewhere about someone doing that and thought it was a fun idea.)

When my sisters were helping my dad pack up our childhood home, they donated my Barbie case (with Barbie, Ken, Skipper, and a Little Kiddle — anybody remember those? — and a full closet of Barbie's clothes, including a Mary Tyler Moore-style hat and even ice skates) to a local church for a tag sale.

Barbie and Ken came in handy decades later — who knew?

"You gave away my Barbie?"

"Ann," my oldest sister said, unsuccessfully trying to contain her shock, because I'm not known as someone who holds on to things, "you wanted to keep your Barbie?"

"Yes!"

They got her and her little family back from the very kind and understanding tag-sale folks. Who knew

Barbie and Ken would come in so handy all those decades later?

Regarding feng shui, no, I don't believe it's the mere state of having two roses in the relationship corner. It was how I felt when I put those roses there, the intention I was setting.

I'm not saying if you put metal in the "helpful people" corner of your house, your whole life will change. But if you clear out the clutter and move into ease and flow, yes, things can change.

With feng shui, it's not the placement of this, there — it's the intention behind it.

I know several people who have or had (they've since passed on) serious health issues; their homes were packed with stuff, and their stuff was coated with dust and grime. It felt like the stuff was holding on to bad energies, and their bodies must've been, too. It's all symbolic and a reflection. As within, so without.

> **Go on a clutter-free diet: house, body, mind.**

You could go on a clutter-free diet: Clean out the clutter in the house, the body (how's your food plan working for you? Are you treating yourself as reverently as you want your partner to?), and your mind. Stingy, low-level, contractive thoughts equal a stingy, low-level, contractive life.

Make room in your home for your beloved — in the bathroom, in the closets, by the bed. Even in the kitchen.

Another true-to-life scenario from my novels is Trish, the shero of *Life in the Hollywood Lane*, as she listens to sappy love songs. I listened to those every night when I drove home from work and was calling in my mate. My workday started and ended a little later than usual, so I usually drove home during the dedication hour.

Speaking of the dedication hour, here was a note to self that I had to remind myself of from time to time: Be so happy for those who are in love (or have a great job, or success in the art you want success in, or whatever). Joy is a much better magnet than wistfulness or, worse, resentment.

Be happy for those who have your dream.

Then came a whole bunch of other ways to get prepared. A long time ago, I heard that when you want a new relationship, buy new lingerie.

Speaker Maru Iabichela once said, "When I moved from a queen-sized bed to a king, I found my king." Life does take us literally sometimes. Make that all times.

I have so many single girlfriends who have pictures and statues of strong, powerful *single* goddesses. That's fine, but they can go in your office, not your living room or bedroom! The bedroom is for couples, pairs, things that come in twos.

Two candles here, two roses there. How about new lingerie and a king-sized bed, too?

BTW, dolphins aren't monogamous, so they're not the best symbol to use if that's what you're after. Swans are a better option, if you want to go animal, as they mate for life.

Back to single things for a moment, another friend had just one chair on her porch. It looked so lonely. I knew she was looking for a partner, so I gently suggested putting out a chair for him. He arrived pretty right quick.

Set out an extra chair on the porch, an extra place at the table.

Rituals for Manifesting

Rev. Karyl Huntley, the author of *Real Life Rituals*, has many suggestions for manifesting. Here are a few of them.

- Use the four elements of earth, air, fire, and water for creating. Possibilities include:

1. Tapping two rocks together in the rhythm of a heartbeat — click-click, click-click — while contemplating your twin flame's heartbeat. That heart is beating out there somewhere, and for a few moments you can allow yourself to hear it.

> **Tune in to the heartbeat of the one who's meant for you.**

2. For air, speak your intention aloud, and let your words be carried to the right places on the breezes.

3. "Fire is the passion that sparks divine activity and moves us toward a goal," Rev. Karyl writes. Place

candles around a room to designate it as sacred space, or release your fears by writing them down and burning the paper.

4. Immerse yourself in water for more fluidity and flexibility as you call in your beloved. You could also release a symbol of something you no longer want in your life into a flowing stream or the sea to wash it away.

Every intention plants a seed.

- Write an intention on a seed and then plant the seed. As you watch it grow and bloom, right before you is the visual representation of your intention also growing and blooming.

- Braid together strands of greenery for an altar or table, putting your intention into every curve of the braid.

She has more ideas, plus she also has rituals for lovers that would be fun once you've found your beloved. (Please see her book in my Recommended Reading list found at the end of this book.)

Steve actually did something similar to the heartbeat ritual. He knew I was out there somewhere, and he tried to tune in to me, my heartbeat, and whatever wild thing I was up to. Somehow he knew I walked on the wild side, he just didn't know *how* wild.

Ann Crawford

What Do You Want to Say to Your Person? Write a Letter

One day I was called to write a letter to this as-yet-unknown twin flame of mine.

November 4, 2005

To my beloved partner, my mate, my best friend,
I keep thinking of the words to that great song — where he knew he loved her before they met, and then he talks about finding and marrying his best friend. At least that's how I remember it, anyway.
I know you're there and that you'll be in my life soon. I give thanks for all the wonderful, wacky, challenging, painful, fun, outrageous, heartbreaking, joyful things that have happened in our lives, bringing us to this place, being the people we are now, ready to love and be loved fully; ready to create a family together; ready to create a home filled with love, light, and laughter; ready to travel a spiritual path with a spiritual powerhouse; ready to work and serve together; ready to laugh and play to-

gether; ready to dance and sing to the music of the spheres together; ready to let go of the past and step into the future together; ready to journey on the adventure of love together.

I already love you. I await you with open arms. I am one of the most loving people you'll ever meet, and I can't wait to wrap this love around you.

Let's boogie!

All my love, always,
Ann

Manifesting is 93% clarity and 7% surrender.

My Manifestation Manual

To me, manifesting is 93 percent clarity and 7 percent surrender. There's that mysteriously magical number again, which has nothing to do with the 93 percent I mentioned to Steve the night before I met him in person. It just happens to be one of my numbers, apparently.

Clarity is *so* important. All these activities, which might seem like way-wacky new-age hogwash to some, helped me get to crystal-clear clarity.

Sometimes a hint comes as a quiet nudge, sometimes it's a thunk.

Steve serendipitously and coincidentally (ha!) saw an ad for eHarmony just under two years after writing out his list. He felt the nudge (thunk) to apply, which took weeks, because he worked on it only at lunchtime.

For the location of women he was open to meeting, he put 100 miles. He was about to click on "finished" when a voice spoke in his head: "Do you really think the woman of your dreams is within 100 miles of Topeka, Kansas?" He clicked on "the world."

He signed up for a whole year. Thanks to synchronicity, I was near the end of a year and was going to take a break, but still had a few days. I received that email saying Steve — Topeka, Kansas, 6'2", 48, a businessman — wants to get in touch with me. I know my state capitals well enough to know that Topeka is the capital of Kansas.

"Been waiting long?"
"Oh, just 48 years."

And, well, you know the rest of the story. Sometimes when he's picking me up somewhere, and I come out of that "somewhere" and find him sitting in the car, I ask, "Been waiting long?"

"Oh, just 48 years," is always the answer to that question. But for many logistical reasons, Steve and I could not have met a minute sooner than we did.

Sometimes your person can't arrive a moment sooner.

A bit more about the list of qualities. I forget where I heard that last one, about the fork, but when I did hear it, I got a big kick out of it and instantly adopted it. I let go of "long hair" until the pandemic came along and Steve grew out his amazing curls.

"Makes me laugh a lot" was far, far more than I ever expected. First thing in the morning to the last thing at night and lots and lots of times in between,

I'm laughing over some silly antic or joke of his.

When he picked me up from the airport, "Thunder Road" was cued up on his car stereo. He hadn't known all the words, but he learned them for me. Both the learning and having it cued up was a class act in my book.

The list is great, of course, as it provides clarity and thus a magnet. But it's just one tool of many. The true magic is in developing it and remaining open to the person being different.

A Letter from the Universe — Actually, It Was from Me

As I mention above, when I was calling in my husband, and people would ask me what I'm looking for, I'd say "a husband, a family, and a home filled with love, light, and laughter." That became my phrase, my mantra.

At the Thanksgiving Eve service at my former spiritual center in California, Rev. Karyl would have us fill out cards for whatever we're thankful for — the following year. My first Thanksgiving in Kansas, an envelope arrived and I pulled out a card. Written in my handwriting was: *I'm living with my husband and family in a home filled with love, light, and laughter.* Wow.

Develop a fun phrase, a special mantra to repeat.

Care to know what wedding present eHarmony sends matches who get married? A crystal bowl from Tiffany's! At least that's what they sent us. I'll never forget my surprise and delight at opening that brown package to find that famous blue Tiffany's box inside. The bowl is lovely, but what really surprised me was that blue box, which let me know where the gift was from.

The Life of Your Love

♥

Kurt says one source of longevity is remaining engaged with each other. We have really different jobs and hobbies, but there's always something we're doing together — sometimes wallpaper removal, sometimes ballroom-dance class. We love Friday nights of two cocktails and a movie. We are a well-oiled machine for hosting gatherings.

Jennie says they have a shared vision of home. In the romantic sense, it means I don't feel at home anyplace that doesn't have Kurt, or home can be anyplace that does have Kurt.

But that isn't just because I love him; it's also because he understands and shares what I need and want in a home. And it's a pretty big list: I have to be free to be me, to be loved and accepted, to have something pretty to look at (but not too much clutter), to always have room for family and friends, and to have stuff to celebrate holidays and milestones, because I am all about that . . . .

And then to be able to say *#%@ it and read a book because I am a chronic *over-scheduler and get tired. We love being home together.*

Jennie & Kurt
Married for 37 years.
They met when she shared
a house with his sister.

♥

Chapter 4
Love Starts Within: The Secret to Becoming the One Who Calls in Your Love

True transformation comes from within. Real spiritual growth doesn't bypass the messy parts — it brings love into them.

♥

We have kept on "working" on our marriage commitment to each other — taking classes to learn best how to love and respect each other, listening to other couples and growing from their struggles and mistakes as well as successes.

We never stop learning to improve, deepening love and respect, maintaining trust, and doing what is best for your spouse at times when you'd like to do what you want to do or go where you want to go. This doesn't mean losing yourself or your opinions, but offering to concede to their preferences if it means you can be together, for example. Just like how you enjoy seeing their face when they open a gift that was well thought out that you know they will love. It's more fun than if you received an expensive gift yourself. It's that joy of pleasing someone else over your own wants/wishes.

Jeanne & Perry
Married for 39 years when he passed.
They met in ballet class.

♥

"It Wasn't Always This Way"

In a Public Relations class I once took, the teacher told us what audiences want to hear the most is this: "Yes, I have this great success in my life now, *but it wasn't always this way.*" The most important information is how you got from there to here, from before to now.

I have to say this loving-relationship propensity of mine wasn't always here; it definitely wasn't always this way. My mom was very sick throughout my childhood and died when I was 17. Despite her being sick, or maybe because of that, we had some very rough times when I was a teenager. She kept the severity of her illness from almost everyone, including me.

But deep down, I probably knew and was reacting to that reality and the fact that it was hidden. The year before she died, we started coming together again, as teens and parents often do. She died before we could truly be friends again, though, and certainly not as two adults.

I watched my mom get swallowed up and defeated by a marriage that didn't serve her well.

I also watched her get swallowed up by a marriage that didn't serve her very well. She wanted to be a nun; my dad talked her out of it with promises of a beautiful life that didn't really come to be for her. I often thought she would've been better off and much happier being a nun (and you'd be sitting here reading someone else's book right now) or at least being with another man. I swore that would never happen to me.

In the years following Mom's death, I was afraid of love. I had a hard time connecting with men, so I went for the ones who were unavailable. I'd also wanted to be a writer, but then turned that off. Or tried to. Writing waited patiently for me to heal a bit.

In my mid-twenties, I took a grief workshop, which helped me heal from the enduring illness and loss of my mother. With that, the on-switch for creative flow was thrown, plus I started becoming interested in men who were available.

I was afraid of love. That often happens with major loss.

I haven't been religious since I was a teen, but I took the workshop at a Catholic-affiliated hospital's community program with some very cool nuns. Maybe in some subconscious way, that was an honoring of my mom's early wish to be one. Actually, I've known many cool nuns.

My dad was an alcoholic. So much for those promising dreams he'd given to Mom. He was also a brilliant engineer, which put him out of reach. The combination of those two things doesn't provide lots of warm fuzzies inside, nor a role model for developing loving relationships.

> **Some of my favorite people are recovering alcoholics.**

Dad stopped drinking when I was in my twenties. Watching him transform into a tender, gracious person was one of the greatest blessings of my life.

He and I took a trip to Yosemite. In the midst of that heart-opening natural splendor, I said to him, "Would you please tell me you love me just the way I am, so I stop looking for that affirmation in every relationship I have?"

Dad turned to me and, with tears in his eyes, said, "I love you exactly the way you are." A year later, I was happily married — no longer searching in the same way.

A conversation like this can take place even if the other person has passed on. I've had conversations like this with my mom. And if it's not possible with someone who is still living, you could have an inner talk with their Higher Self. This is for you.

We can have those long-desired conversations, even if they have to be in another form.

Before that meeting and marriage happened, though, I'd gotten into recovery for my own addictions. Could you imagine if I hadn't done that? Whatever relationship I got in wouldn't have been very strong or good.

I have a friend who would put "420 friendly" on her online dating profile. When she finally quit smoking pot, she said, "Thank goodness I didn't meet anybody when I had that on there!"

I also had tons and tons of therapy and twelve-step meetings. It took a *lot* of work to turn me into what one former boyfriend called me: "Someone who has love oozing from every cell."

♥

We both decided years ago that if either of us left, we'd be taking our biggest problems with us and leaving our best friend behind!

Connie & Gary
Married for 45 years.
They met at work, a bookstore.

♥

Divorcing the Dream

When I was much younger, I always found it super annoying that we can't get a great job unless we have a job. But then we can't really get a relationship until we're out of the one we're in. That's not always the case, of course; I know many couples who have met their current spouses while they were in a previous marriage.

Sometimes that's just the way the timing needs to be. But, overall, if we have to clear out space in our homes for this beautiful being, we certainly have to clear out space in our lives and heal from the pain of that breakup.

What most people grieve isn't the person — it's the loss of the dream.

As I mention above, I knew my ex-husband and I had outgrown each other long before we broke up. But I still loved him, and always will. Also, to be honest about something I really don't want to admit, I thought what I had to abide was far more tolerable than the two years of excruciating pain, it's been said, it takes to recover from a divorce.

The pain wasn't all that bad . . . except when it was. It certainly wasn't continuous for two years. I'd say it got really agonizing around our wedding anniversary, about eleven months after we broke up. We always did a very special event to celebrate us, and when that day came and went without us doing it, I really knew in my heart — and not just my mind anymore —it was over.

> **The pain wasn't all that bad — except when it was.**

However, I drove by the adorable inn where we got married and would always stay on our anniversary. There was a light on in the room that'd become "ours," starting on our wedding night. (No stalker here: the inn was on my way home, and I could see the room's window from the nearby two-lane highway.)

I was surprised to find myself so happy to see that light, knowing people were in there enjoying that darling room. I hoped they were having as good a time as we did . . . well, not counting our last time there, a month before we broke up. (Another sign.) But the light showed life moves on.

The mourning came around in waves and circles, as grief does. It also cracked my heart wide open in compassion for people going through similar or worse life events. And it came to an end.

Divorce is not a failure at all.

What a lot of people grieve is the loss of the dream. They also grieve for the perceived failure.

I repeat, divorce is not a failure at all in my book. It's hard to grow at the same pace. I have two chums from college who've been together since then, and that's fabulous . . . and unusual that two such dynamic, powerful people have grown together in such compatible ways.

> **Growing together at the same rate isn't always possible.**

The late comedian Bob Newhart joked that in the Midwest, people date events by what age their kids were. For example, "Oh, yeah, Bobby was going into middle school when they built the new shopping center." In California, however, he said people date events by who they were married to. "Oh, yeah, I was married to Holly when the new shopping center went up."

I know a lot of people — and not just in California — who've been divorced; I also know a lot of people who've stayed together. I've heard that some folks say if they knew then what they know now, they would've stayed with their first spouse. I'll always love my ex-husband for the things I loved him for in the first place. But it doesn't mean we should still be together.

Recently someone asked in a big Facebook group, "Have you ever broken up with someone you were still in love with?"

I answered, "Yes, and it was the best thing I ever did. Actually, I've done that several times. I just knew that wonderful man I was in love with at the time wasn't the one for the long term."

What the Most Eligible Singles Say

For me, the worst moments of being single were Sunday mornings. Plus, I remember reading an article in a San Francisco paper long ago that interviewed the "most eligible" singles in town. They asked what's the best and worst part of being solo. One person answered the same for both: "Quiet evenings at home."

Bypass Spiritual Bypassing

I know I said that a powerful manifesting agent is joy for another's success, whether in career or in love. In our spiritual bypassing world, though, we don't always have to jump to that. It's okay to feel sad — fully, deeply — and even say, "Why not me, too?"

Spiritual bypassing is when we use spiritual ideas, positive thinking, or "love and light" to avoid feeling or dealing with something uncomfortable. It's basically saying, "I'm fine, it's all Divine" when what's really needed is to sit down with the grief, anger, fear, or truth that's trying to get our attention.

It's avoiding the inner work by wrapping ourselves in a sparkling, spiritual blanket. It can sound like:

- "I shouldn't be angry — I'm spiritual."
- "I don't want to focus on the negative."
- "Everything happens for a reason" — said too early, before the heart has time to catch up.
- "If I just stay high vibe, the hard stuff will disappear."

When you integrate rather than avoid, you become clearer, truer, more magnetic.

But the truth is, real spiritual growth isn't about skipping the messy parts. *It's about bringing love into them.* When you integrate rather than avoid, you become clearer, truer, more magnetic, and far more aligned with the love you're calling in.

About Those Statistics . . .

Okay, back to manifesting our true love. A friend once said the next time she meets someone, she's going to have him fill out a questionnaire. I said, "That's what online dating is — a questionnaire in the form of their profile."

One couple, who eventually married, both lied on their online profiles. At least they had that in common.

This isn't an advertisement for online dating in general or eHarmony in particular, but . . . a friend had set an intention for many years. She kept drawing the Harmony card from her Tarot deck *every single time*, which led her to sign up for eHarmony. Yep, signs come from all over.

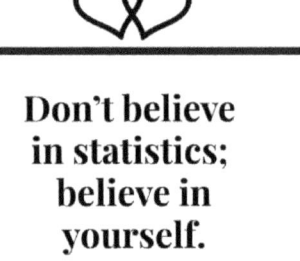

Don't believe in statistics; believe in yourself.

At an age when, statistically speaking, it was more likely to be struck by lightning than find love, she did meet the man who became her husband — at her church. She went to the eight AM service and he went to the noon, though, so they weren't going to meet there without some divine intervention (hehe). Her message? Right here:

♥

Never believe in statistics, believe in yourself. I would offer that intentions are powerful, even when you're not seeing immediate results. Lots of things had to happen before we came together.

Diane & Harv
Married for 13 years.
They met through eHarmony.

♥

My Answer

And here's my very flip answer when people ask for the secret of how Steve and I stay so happily married: Steve is *really* easygoing. Hah!

But the answer for both of us is pacing has a lot to do with it. We don't mean pacing just in, for example, one likes to sleep in on weekends and the other likes to get up at 5 AM to go climb a mountain; we also mean pacing in neatness, exercise, success orientation, and multitudes of things like that.

My answer to the secret of our happy marriage? Steve is *really* easygoing, ROFL.

We both put up with quite a few things. (Topeka, Kansas? Really? Actually, it's quite a great place.) I have to be at the ocean every few months. He doesn't eat organic like I do. I had a boyfriend chide me for eating a non-organic banana once (what? it has a thick peel), so I give Steve a huge berth for his food choices because I know how awful it feels to be chided.

I worked with a nutritionist for a bit. Her husband doesn't do organic either. I asked her how she handles that, and she said, "I'd rather be married than right."

We all know how well it works when someone tries to change us; it works just as well when we try to change others. If something a potential partner does is a complete non-negotiable for you, though, look elsewhere instead of waiting for a change of behavior.

♥

You're going to fight, so you have to learn how to do it well. What do you ultimately want as the end result?

Karri & Mark
Married for 32 years.
Met at a comedy club
and they're still laughing.

♥

Honestly, I know most people, including professionals, say talking in person is the best thing. But Steve and I fight best through text! We both feel fully heard, and we both have an opportunity to say everything we want without feeling rushed in the heat of the moment. We also don't get triggered as much. Hey, it works for us. The heartfelt conversation comes after that.

You're going to fight — so learn how to do it well.

My parents lived by the maxim to never go to bed angry. It didn't really work for them, though; my mother just pushed everything inward. Besides, being overtired might be 95 percent of the reason the fight is happening.

One thing my former husband used to love to say (and I loved to hear) when people say, "Oh, we never fight," was, "What are you afraid to say to each other?"

BTW, on the opposite-of-fighting side of things, this is for the multitudes of partners who want to "fix it" — whatever "it" they think needs fixing right then. Sometimes we other partners just need a kind, understanding "Honey," or whatever endearment or pet name is used.

Translated, that's, "I love you, I hear you, I get it." We just want to know we're heard and commiserated with for the moment.

> "The true purpose of marriage is to heal our childhood wounds."
> ~Harville Hendrix
> Author of
> *Getting the Love You Want*

I love how Arielle and Brian, in the first long-time married-couples' contribution in this book, quote Harville

Hendrix: "The true purpose of marriage is to heal our childhood wounds." They go on to say that having a partner who is "open, willing, and a safe place to land provides the greatest healing possible." As I say earlier, the true, full healing of whatever has hurt us can take a long, long time — even a lifetime.

♥

Have two bathrooms and a spare bedroom, for those nights when one of you can't sleep and is tossing and turning. That way you won't keep the other one up. Have a commitment to personal growth and honesty. Call each other on your stuff.

Sally & Eric
Married for 37 years.
They met while doing
their spiritual practice.

♥

Summary

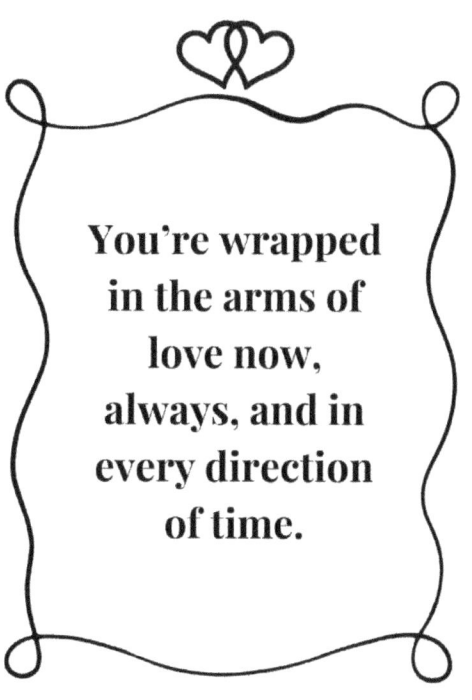

You're wrapped in the arms of love now, always, and in every direction of time.

To me, as I mention above, manifesting is 93 percent clarity and 7 percent surrender. Clarity is vital — and I include all the action steps in that 93-percent part, because they help get to the clarity.

And as I say in the feng shui section, it's not the action of planting seeds or getting the roses or whatever . . . it's the intention, the announcement, behind doing so. And buying the lingerie isn't telling the Universe we're ready — it's telling ourselves. The Universe already knows.

Arriving at Clarity

I include my list for general manifesting in Chapter 2. To summarize on how to get to that 93-percent clarity, here's another list that's not quite as detailed, but has some overall ideas on possible actions to take. This list is also not borrowed, also very lived.

1. Clear your stuff and heal your wounds as much as possible — both in the psyche and in the

heart. Heal the anger. This might take a while.

2. Write a list of exactly what you want . . . but go for the feeling, not the picture. What shows up may be even better than anything you could have imagined.

3. Become all the things on said list yourself. This might take a while, too. You already know how, though. Then you become the magnet; that's what draws them in.

When you become the traits you want in your partner, you become the magnet.

4. Feng shui the holy Moses out of it all: two red roses, two wine glasses, two swans, two red

candles, Barbie and Ken in their wedding apparel — whatever occurs to you.

5. Take steps that show yourself you're ready: Buy lingerie. Get that king-sized bed. Ignite the spark of love by lighting that pair of red candles, with sacred intention. Make room in the closet, around the bed and the house, and throughout your life. Being too busy won't bring in your beloved.

6. Don't put any part of your life on hold while waiting for a relationship. You can buy your dream home, take that dream vacation, and do the things you want to do now — including getting your finances in shape if some of those dreams are out of reach for the time being.

7. Be enjoying such a full, great life that a relationship is the aforementioned rose on top of the icing on the cake. You don't need it, but hey, wouldn't that

be great? Meanwhile, you're traveling, going to art shows, volunteering, basically participating in whatever activities you love to do. We can have what we want when we don't *have* to have it to feel fulfilled. And everything doesn't have to be perfect — just joy-filled . . . and spacious enough to hold more.

We usually get what we want when it doesn't *have* to happen for us to be happy.

8. Be happy and grateful for what is, now. If that's really hard, start small: the sunshine, the neighbor's rosebush, a job that pays the bills, a smile from the doctor's receptionist.

9. Have a praise phrase or mantra you love repeating, one that makes your heart sing.

10. Acceptance . . . don't expect your beloved to come with *all* the specifications. Shed judgment. Know that compromises come with the territory.

11. Feel all feelings, fully. "This really stinks!" is a good starter. But don't dwell there. Don't resent anyone for having what you want; be happy for their success. Their having it means you can have it, too.

Feel all feelings, fully. "This really stinks!" is a great starting place.

12. Surrender. This doesn't mean giving up — it means handing over the steering wheel to something wiser than our worry. It's that moment when you've done your inner work, planted the seeds, tended the soil . . . and now you let the Universe do Its part. Surrender allows you to loosen your grip on the timeline, release the "how" and "when," and choose trust over tension. It's saying, "I'm ready, I'm open, and I'm willing to be surprised."

Surrender is handing over the steering wheel to something wiser than our worry.

When you surrender, you stop forcing and you start allowing, which is exactly when love can slip in through the side door you didn't even know was there.

Getting Lucky

There is some luck, too, I have to admit. "You're just the right amount of odd," Steve once said to me.

That's a *lot* of luck, actually. Most people would think I'm quite odd, LOL.

"You're just the right amount of odd."

This Happened

Of the myriad things I did to call in my love, one of the most powerful and palpable was this small ritual. One night — March 21, 2006, to be exact — I felt very clear this was the time to call him in.

One of my dearest friends and I sat in her living room, lit candles, and spoke the intention out loud. I felt the presence of "my guy" for the first time. I found myself slow dancing with someone just a few inches taller — buff, with broad shoulders. Slow dancing has turned out to be one of our things.

Steve is the size and build of the man in that . . . experience. It was far more than a fantasy. It felt closer to a premonition. The first time we danced together (like, in the same time zone, even in the very same room, haha), it felt familiar. A return.

March 21 is his birthday. We were matched exactly three months later. It couldn't have happened a moment earlier, as you know from before. But when the time was right, there it was. There we were. Here we are.

Ann Crawford

Hold on to Your Dreams; Let Go of the How and What It'll All Look Like

Steve and I could've both dismissed that seemingly crazy hit to sign up for eHarmony. I could've stayed in my little hippie surfer town.

At our wedding celebration, I said, "If I told anyone in this room I was going to travel the world (again) or climb Mt. Everest or the like, they would've just said, 'Yeah, that's Ann.' But when I said I was moving to Topeka, Kansas, to get married to a man I just met and be a stepmom to two teenagers, well . . . ." Everyone laughed.

So, we can always hold on to our dreams, but definitely let go of the how and what it'll look like. That about sums it all up.

The love each of us looked *with* allowed us to receive the love that was waiting for us.

Steve and I absolutely held on to the dream of true love, and we released any attachment to the how and the appearances. (Again, Kansas? Really? Sure!)

The love each of us looked *with* allowed us to receive the love that was waiting for us. And we were married six months after we were matched, on 12/21 — when the one became two and the two became one.

A friend asked, in reference to the love-interest part of my stories, "Which one of your books is about Steve?"

"He's inspired all of them since we came together," was my answer.

Unexpected Gifts and Everyday Celebrations

I recently said to Steve, "This is the most me I've ever met." He gives me so much space to just be me in all my fullness, no holding back anywhere. And likewise. What a gift. And the gifts just keep showing up, big and small, once or ongoing.

I once heard the suggestion to decide which morning task you enjoy least, and do it the night before. I told Steve, "I can't do that because it'd be undoing the deadbolt." I can't explain myself; I just don't like doing that.

But ever since I mentioned it, the deadbolt is opened for me every morning. And a very tall elf washes his breakfast bowl. The little acts can be so big.

We still do a slow dance every time one of us leaves the house. That's almost 20 years of that sweetness, which we both then take out into our day and to the people we encounter. I bet they can sense it.

You can create your own loving celebrations, too — even for yourself, in the meantime.

Whenever I return home, he's waiting in the driveway to greet me (perfect timing thanks to the map app) and to hear what love song I'm playing for him. That's my favorite moment of the day. You can create your own loving celebrations, too — even for yourself, in the meantime.

Here's to the Life of Your Love Happening for You

When I first told Steve I was thinking of writing this book, he said, "There's nothing higher you could do. It's your highest calling — to help others find their love, too."

I am so crazy honored to be writing a book about finding the love of your life. And nothing makes me more grateful for Steve than to be able to write this, to make this statement.

And if it happened for us and many others we know, it can happen for you.

Ann Crawford

You already are the love. Here's to you and your cherished, splendiferous life to wrap your arms of love around.

Just for the record, you're wrapped in the arms of love when you're born, you're wrapped in the arms of love when you die, you're wrapped in the arms of love now, you're wrapped in the arms of love always.
You don't need to look for love. Love is what you look with. *It's all that you are. Love of another is just the recognition of this love.*

—from *Angels on Overtime*

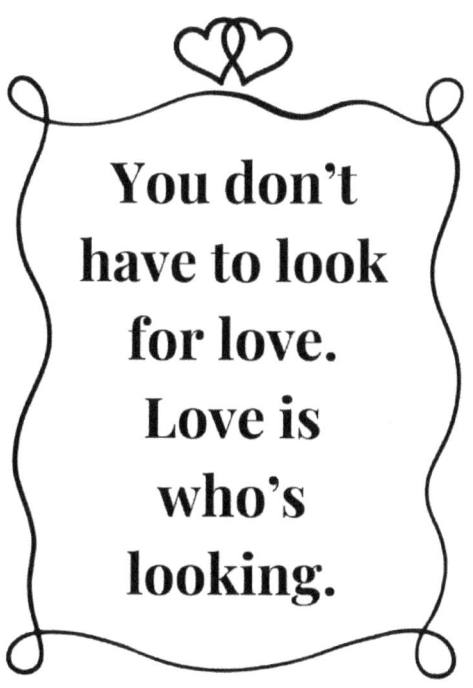

You don't have to look for love. Love is who's looking.

Appendix

Here's something for fun: our eHarmony profiles. The lines in bold were prompts from the site, followed by our responses. These became the About Steve and About Ann pages.

Steve said that the one thing he is most passionate about is: music.

The three things he is most thankful for are: my kids (I know, that's two things), my love of music, my spirituality.

The most influential person in Steve's life has been: the author Joel Goldsmith. Because of his books, I became seriously interested in learning about and rapidly growing my spirituality.

Steve's friends describe him as: intelligent, easygoing, perceptive, and optimistic.

Three of Steve's best life skills are: continuing to expand my knowledge and awareness, raising and/or caring for children, remaining calm yet resilient during a crisis.

The most important thing Steve is looking for in a person is: her passion for learning about growing within and enjoying her life.

The first thing you'll probably notice about Steve when you meet him is: my easygoing nature. I have the ability to get along with anyone, at any time.

The one thing Steve wishes more people would notice about him is: my ability to see the big picture.

Steve typically spends his leisure time: with my kids, enjoying doing just about anything with them. Listening to and performing music.

The things Steve can't live without are: my kids, music, spirituality, books, family.

The last book Steve read and enjoyed is: *Friendship with God* by Neale Donald Walsch. It broadened my understanding of things.

And there was his photo. My first response to that was the kindness in those big, brown eyes. His hair was way too short, though, LOL. It hasn't been that short again as long as I've known him, but it didn't get as long as I really like until the pandemic hit, as I mention, hehe. Of course, if the guy truly for me was bald, that'd be fine, too.

Here are my answers.

The one thing Ann is most passionate about is: Doing my part in making the world a better place, everything from doing my inner work to make me a better person to doing all I can to serve humanity. I love to think big.

The three things which Ann is most thankful for are: my family, friends, and spiritual community; my wonderful health and vitality; seeing love and beauty everywhere I look, because I've learned to look for it.

The most influential person in Ann's life has been: Michael B. Beckwith, Agape International Spiritual Center. He has taken his talents and life purpose and allows himself to be used by Life to serve everyone. He doesn't talk about his own greatness, but the innate greatness in each one of us and how important it is to express that greatness in the world for the benefit of all.

Ann's friends describe her as: happy, passionate, spiritual, and romantic.

Three of Ann's best life skills are: creating a peaceful, beautiful home environment, finding and taking on challenging activities, making new friends.

The most important thing Ann is looking for in a person is: my ideal mate loves life, has a positive outlook, and is a spiritual powerhouse. He is awake and aware of the connection of all life. He is passionate and romantic. He has done his work and is ready to give and receive love fully. He's very attractive and healthy and takes good care of himself. He already has and/or is looking to create a family. He loves to laugh. He knows all the words to "Thunder Road." (Just kidding — not a necessity, but you know what I mean.)

The first thing you'll probably notice about Ann when you meet her is: lots of people notice that I'm happy, bright, and shining except when I'm not, which isn't often.

The one thing Ann wishes more people would notice about her is: Hmmmmmm . . . I am pretty much right out there, in a quiet way, not loud, so I don't think there's anything in this category.

Ann typically spends her leisure time: walking my dog on the cliffs overlooking a nearby beach, watching sunsets, going to movies, watching a few select funny TV shows, hiking, going out to parties and special events, going to plays and concerts, traveling, or staying home by the fireplace.

Ann Crawford

The things Ann can't live without are: friends, especially a special best friend/partner; spiritual community and paths; work that is in service to humanity; a beautiful, comfortable, nurturing home; a dog; a sense of humor; travel.

The last book Ann read and enjoyed is: I just read *Testimony of Light* by Helen Greaves. Two dear friends, who were nuns, had a telepathic relationship; when one died, their relationship continued. The one who passed on described her new existence as completely based on her thoughts and actions, which is how things work here, but it's far more noticeable on the other side. I am reading *The Field* now, which is scientific evidence of what metaphysicians have always known — that everything is related and affects everything else. If you think this is bunk or Greek, then it probably wouldn't work with us.

One thing that only Ann's best friends know is: Become my best friend and find out! (It's funny.) :)

(Note from the future here: What I was thinking of was my hilarious imitation of Lucille Ball/Lucy Ricardo's wailing.)

Some additional information Ann wanted you to know is: I . . . am left of liberal . . . do a lot of volunteer work including humanitarian work overseas . . . have been around the world twice, including some very off-the-beaten-track places . . . meditate and I'm a spiritual counselor for my church, which is a metaphysical/new thought denomination . . . don't drink or do drugs; I don't mind if you drink a little bit, but no drug takers please . . . that is a recent photo . . . I am open to relocating. If you're not the man for me, I wish you the very best in finding the woman for you

Forgiveness Meditation

The audio version of this meditation can be found at anncrawford.net/forgiveness-meditation.

Imagine a time before this time — a time of love and connection, when you knew with all your being that you were loved. This is a time before now, maybe even before birth. Maybe it's a time as a child, first feeling the awe of creation on a beautiful day out in nature. Maybe it's the first feeling of love: the rush of joy from seeing your beloved. Maybe it's the first time you knew you were one with Love, with Life. This Love fills you, surrounds you, is you.

Imagine this time, this time called right now. Bring this Love into this moment, now. In this loving place, think of someone who needs your forgiveness. This someone perhaps erred on the human level, and you haven't yet released the bind of resentment. See yourself tethered to this person with a cord. See the cord grow taut as you try to pull away from them, and then slacken as you accept their tie to you. Now see the cord start to glow, a golden rope of light. As the cord glows brighter and brighter, see it start to disintegrate. The cord falls away, leaving only a trace of light between you and the other. You are no longer tethered to this person, only connected by light, in great love.

Imagine a time after this time. A time of love and connection. You see this person. You thank them for all they have taught you. They no longer hold you bound. You are free.

Feel this moment again, a sacred time of love and connection. Feel the miracle of Life, alive in you right now, coursing through every cell and fiber in your body. Feel the Love, feel the gratitude of knowing and remembering.

Recommended Reading

The Soulmate Secret by Arielle Ford
[1]Whenever I quote a suggestion from a couple in this book, I tell how they met, except for Arielle and Brian . . . please read Arielle's book to discover this — it's an amazing and beautiful story.

Calling in the One by Katherine Woodward Thomas

    I can't recommend the above two books highly enough. They are chockablock with exercises to help heal the past, remove blocks, and move ahead more extensively than was my aim in *The Life of Your Love.* If you find you need more help in clearing away the past, these two books are goldmines.

How to Not Die Alone by Logan Ury

Real Life Rituals by Rev. Karyl Huntley

Care of the Soul and *Soul Mates* by Thomas Moore

For further spiritual teachings, I highly recommend any of the books and recordings by Anita Moorjani, Barbara Marx Hubbard, Deepak Chopra, Joel Goldsmith, Michael B. Beckwith, and Thich Nhat Hanh. The list could go on and on, but these are my favorites.

Acknowledgements

First and foremost on my list of acknowledgments is the love of my life and the life of my love. Steve, I adore you. And I'll keep saying it: you are truly the best thing that ever, ever happened to me.

I often say it's one of the honors of my life to do this or that — make that documentary about Vietnam veterans or travel the globe for a world-peace project. But I've never before said it is *the* honor of my life to do one particular thing. Writing this book — on this topic, and sincerely meaning it —definitely is the honor of my life.

I could only write about it by living it first. And living as someone who *can* write this book is the greatest gift of my life.

Sure, there have been moments that weren't all sunshine and roses. But our commitment to each other and to what we've created together has always prevailed.

I love what we have here: a super fun romcom with profound depth and spectacular heights, plus a really great soundtrack, LOL.

As a bass player, you always say the guitar gets people singing, but the bass gets people dancing. It has been and is one of the greatest joys of my life to dance through this world with you. I even said "let's boogie" in the letter I wrote to you seven months before we met, and look at us now . . . still dancing every day.

Thank you to eHarmony as well as our former spouses, who taught us so much and got us ready for each other.

Thank you to my editor, Diane Bishop, and to Christie Buchele for her awesome social media coaching as well as being a most outstanding comedy coach and teacher.

Overflowing love and thanks to my special peeps: Angela, Arielle, Ariyana, Ashanta, Barbara, Betsey, Chris, Dana, Deb, Grace, Joan, Karyl, Kathleen, Kylee, Lavandar, Lisa, Melainah, Patrice, Sabine, Tammie, Valentine, Vikki, and Veronica.

The Life of Your Love

And more overflowing love and thanks to my beloved Guy, Kim, Liz, Marion, Sue, and Suzanne, plus my special angels Lee, Mary, Sherry, and my parents, who loved me into being.

Thank you to the generous contributors of suggestions and ideas: Arielle Ford and Brian Hilliard, Barbara Marx Hubbard, Betsey and George, Connie and Gary, Diane and Harv, Jeanne and Perry, Jim Self, Karen and Paul, Karri and Mark, Rev. Karyl Huntley and Paul, Rev. Katherine Revoir, Revs. Lloyd Strom and Marcia Sutton, Maru Iabichela, Maya and Luis, Michael B. Beckwith, Nicki Scully, Peter Tork, Sally and Eric, Stephen and Rob, Sue and Steve, and Thich Nhat Hanh. Some of these folks are no longer with us, but their teachings will always be.

To these gifted groups and artists, my gratitude: Bread; Bruce Springsteen; Bruno Mars; Bryan Adams; Carlos Santana; Earth, Wind & Fire; Ed Sheeran; Enya; Eric Clapton; Foreigner; Gladys Knight & The Pips; Joe Cocker; John Denver; John Legend; Led Zeppelin; Lonestar; Mark Knopfler and

Emmylou Harris; Neil Young; Sam Smith; and The Stylistics. Even Elvis.

That's quite the mix! They composed the playlist for this book, which is by far my favorite of all of my book playlists, since I love love songs, as you well know by now.

My final thanks go to you, dear reader: thank you so much for being part of the journey of *The Life of Your Love*. If any of my experiences or ideas here help you call in the love of your life or add to your days at all, I'm beyond happy. So much love to you.

Books by Ann Crawford

Contemporary Fiction

BAZOOMERANGS
Amazon Best Seller

A tale about three generations of women — a transgender daughter, her Trumper mom, and her still-a-flower-child grandmother — all living under one roof. What could go right?

Amazon review: "BAZOOMERANGS is more than a family drama — it's a celebration of love, resilience, and the bonds that unite us across generational and personal differences. Crawford skillfully mixes humor with deeper explorations of self-discovery and growth, making this book both entertaining and deeply moving."

Ann Crawford

LIFE IN THE HOLLYWOOD LANE
Amazon Best Seller

Quirky-crazy, sometimes humorous jaunt through an actor's recovery after her BFF's suicide.

NetGalley review: "One of the most moving books I have ever read . . . beautifully written story that will stay with you long after you've read the last page."

Alternative & Visionary

FRESH OFF THE STARSHIP
Amazon Best Seller
Readers' Favorite Book Award Winner

In this romantic comedy, a starbeing was supposed to travel light-years across the universe to help humanity by working in Washington, D.C. — but she accidentally lands in a small Kansas town in the body of Missy. Join her on this whimsical journey as she discovers the beauty of life and love on Earth.

Reader's Favorite Review: "5 stars! A light and enjoyable adventure that comments on human nature and the beauty of our world . . . . Very funny, but it was the wider ethos of the tale that really grabbed me. Overall, a brighter look at life today that is sure to keep you smiling from page to page."

SPELLWEAVER

Mystical journey with a healer during the Burning Times in Scotland.

The Feathered Quill Review: "This tale holds on to the reader and never lets go . . . . The characters and subplots [are] intoxicating . . . . The author has cast her own remarkable 'spell' upon readers with this unforgettable tale."

ANGELS ON OVERTIME
Amazon Best Seller
Feathered Quill and
Reader's Favorite Book Award Winner

Although meant to be together, life keeps getting in the way of two lonely hearts — that is, until their angels begin working overtime.

Amazon review: "This is the funniest, most enjoyable, and most delightfully irreverent spiritual novel I've ever read. I couldn't stop laughing."

MARY'S MESSAGE:
An Alternative History of Mary Magdalene and Jesus

The untold love story between the Bible's two most powerful characters.

Amazon review: "It's a gentle but powerful reminder of the power of love."

Non-fiction

THE LIFE OF YOUR LOVE:
Calling in the Love of Your Life

Ready to call in the love of your life? Here's a luminous guide to finding (and becoming) the kind of partner your soul has always longed for. This warm, humorous, and deep book reminds you that love isn't something you chase — it's something you live.

VISIONING:
Creating the Life of Our Dreams and a World That Works for Us All

Step-by-step guidance on how you can create the life of your wildest dreams, a life that serves yourself and humanity, the life you were born to live.

Barbara Marx Hubbard review: "*Visioning* speaks to our heart, mind, and spirit with a delightful, lyrical, and wise guidance to help us shift from the separated to the divine self that we really are."

About the Author

Ann Crawford is an award-winning author and filmmaker, eternal optimist, world traveler, and lifelong lover of love. She writes about joy, connection, overcoming adversity, as well as the wild and wonderful adventure of this being-human ride.

Ann lives in Colorado with her husband, who keeps her laughing every single day — and still makes her heart skip a beat.

Visit anncrawford.net to learn more or connect with her on Instagram:

@anncrawfordauthor
@thelifeofyourlove

www.ingramcontent.com/pod-product-compliance
Lightning Source LLC
LaVergne TN
LVHW051216070526
838200LV00063B/4928